# The Uninvited Bridge Line

Greg Moser

Presentation by *BookLeaf Publishing*

Web: www.bookleafpub.com

E-mail: info@bookleafpub.com

ISBN: 9789357692069

First edition 2022

# DEDICATION

For Emily.

Always supportive, always there.

# ACKNOWLEDGEMENT

All my love and gratitude to my wife, Emily. You are always so caring, as I work to find my voice and present it to the world. You inspire me every day to be the best that I can be.

A huge thank you goes to everyone that has supported my writing this year. Publishing Bruised Orange was a huge leap of faith for me, and the feedback from all of you has reinforced that I made the right decision to share my work with the world. I hope you enjoy this new collection.

Lastly, a big thank you to my friend that invited me to participate in this writing challenge. This project came with no preparation on my part, and it got my ideas flowing again after some time off. I am very happy with how this collection turned out, and I appreciate you inviting me to be a part of this. Thanks, AP.

# Behind The Mask

Behind the mask
We all wear in the now
A buffer against unwanted droplets entering.
Mixed, confused emotions easier to conceal.
Sometimes you have to judge a friend's eyes
When you ask "How do you really feel?"

The mask with the double-meaning
Protect and conceal.
What is necessary
And what is real
I don't mind wearing one today
Just please do not inquire
What I have to say.

If life should one day return
I'll say goodbye to the mask
Hello again to normal
Prepare to show my face
My sometimes-sullen expressions.
Go back to my day-to-day
My multitude of life's lessons.

# Deserted Lot

Pulling into the deserted lot
The moon providing a tender, uneasy light
This awkward Saturday night dance
Of work. And misery. And curiosity.
Events that inexplicably came together by
chance
All swirled into this near-satisfying moment.

Senses at heightened vulnerability-
Given the late-night visit
Coinciding with the calendar's march
And the unrelenting fatigue
Of the last 24 hours
That were anything but rest.

Walking slowly, yet with deliberate resolve.
A destination deserted, but an end within
the grasp of hands dried out
From stress, rather than the seasonal pre-winter
air looming over my shoulder.

Protect me on this late October night
As I celebrate- silently. Alone in a building
normally full of purpose
No desire for masks nor celebration
Just want to complete my required duties
Rid myself of this awkward sensation.

# Day Old Doughnuts

Day old doughnuts often satisfy the soul
Assist us as we face another routine morning
Keep the motions running while the mind
gingerly loses control.
Discarded for a fresher alternative
By the unassuming, self-centered date police
Give them my attention
Sell me your smile and I'll share with you
              a piece.

What is fresh and inviting today
May be gone without words tomorrow
Forgotten or ignored
Commerce left to wallow.
More than that.  Always.
A deeper meaning than age or appearance
could ever truly express.
Give them more than a passing glance
A complicated medium yearning to be
understood.

# Pawns For The Selfish

They exist like the everyday dust
that greets the casual observer
Pawns for the selfish
Their spirit dimmed, but for a moment
Seize the promise that any half of Opportunity
may whisper

The desire to travel, feel the unusual sensation
Those brief moments of freedom can bring
Yet the selfish present their ill-advised
justifications
Smile while analyzing the root of the sting.

And then the rain came.
Not the usual, predictable tears.
True, heavy floods of relief.
The timing more than a perfect moment
That could've been planned with purpose.
Beauty.  Between 2 uninspiring moments.
The pawns had their moment
While the clouds provided pause.

# Another Mile

Exhausted
Little left after exiting the stage.
Will my rest be fruitful and satisfying
Or is it simply the lonely byproduct of age?
Head up to the clouds if asked to go a mile
Pretend it's challenging, yet satisfying
Halt briefly and give a smile.

My will- tested and bested
Always firm, yet fragile
A step to the right
Avoid that awkward, familiar fight.
Go the distance.  It's been encouraged before.
For the miles have been confusingly long
Worked at times for my voice to be heard
Turned it to 11 til my song was audible.
Help and fairness
All that was asked.
Curiously ignored.

Dress up these laces and head out again
Another mile logged.
If the world turns in wonder,
It is all that was required.
If the path appears endlessly uphill

Expectations are exceeded.  My own.
Outside opinions in the rear view
As the miles continue to curve
Look sparingly at the path.

# Collapsing Sensations

The room collapsed
with a swift motion.
In her mind.
The panic that began to consume her face
Told the story- without words.
Her lips felt numb, yet exposed no weakness.
A tale not to be heard.
That spinning sensation crept in again.
No need for the safety of sleep
Or to pick up the phone and call a friend.

# Wash Twice

Let me sleep
For my mind is bloated
Yet my thoughts are mine to keep.
Tomorrow will arrive in hours
To turn the page on the forgettable
As I clear my space and take stock.
Fighting the urge to stop and stare
What say you, clock?

Be gone this day
Wish it were so simple for the mind
Jaded thoughts still led astray.

Wash me twice and call me clean.
The world shall not notice
What I heard or thought I'd seen.
For I'd stay silent if inquiry was made
It was genuine, so much more than a dream.

I will wake when my soul is prepared
Brought to the shadows of the ceiling
When my heart is again giving.
This rest is for the self-centered side.
Retreat to the meadow
Do you think I can hide?

Go seek the shelter and call in the doctor
No magic potion to dispense this visit
Just the head and the hands to dive in.
Swim to the center
Find the purpose tomorrow.

# Clarity

Geena gave Dante a single rose
His reaction was indifference.
For reasons not audible.
Her hurt ran deep
Could not function
                    nor sleep.

A singular gesture straight from her mother's
garden
The jungle of roses that co-existed with the
wildflowers of yesterday.

Unable to mumble to him- not a single word
Her expression of discontent and pain
Was what his heart finally heard.

To see the light,
Make it right
Dante shifted his pride.
From himself and his shortcomings as a person.
He held her hand and stroked her thick,
tri-colored hair
Tried as he could to calm her fragile nerves
Speak in a simple, soulful way that he was
genuine- where she sought clarity.

# 20 Minutes

The wheels on the black bus turned
Slowly and deliberately
Until confidence crept in.
All it took was movement.
Suddenly, everything was rolling again-
Especially the mood.
Gone the sudden, salty-water-sass.
Replaced by the taste, the promise
That this shall pass and brighter
Beginnings are near.

The fresh, unseasonably warm air
Aided us both.
Wish I'd thought of it sooner.
Tricked by the wind into thinking
Another lost day was ahead.
But here we are, our backs to the basement
The open, snowless road ahead.
Don't forget your helmet- or me.
If only I could keep up.
And more days could be like this-
These twenty minutes.

# Waves

The waves watched her bend
In ways foreign, even to their everlasting spirit.
It was her resiliency fighting to learn
What was responsible and (or) respectable
To blend with the bland she found
surrounding her spirit.
Too many new souls to count- all with defined
timelines.
Here they were-
Experts ready to dissect her failures.
Her strength in these times- understated.
Fighting through her multiple shortcomings
Afraid to make the call.
Bending into the woman she knew she craved in
this moment.
Satisfaction.  And loathing.
No need for a private eye to research this
transformation.
All but complete
Expectations determined to meet.
Her own.

# Flower

Flower-
will you still be here tomorrow
Shine in your hour?
Show a fresh scent to the uninvited
Begin to question the seeds from which you
sprang?

Oh flower, please be genuine.
I do not desire your plastic imposter
Crave true feelings
Not fake plastic symbols
That fear not the seasons.

Flower, make me real.
Invite the sunshine with its rays of redemption
Make us whole
While emotions take their toll.
Give me the scents to survive the endless night
ahead
If you should wilt before I can react
I'll work tirelessly to bring you from the dead.
Never mind the meddling robins of the hour
Cannot trust a hopeless, foolish bird
That claims the ground has gone despairingly
sour.

# Shine On

Dust kicking
Room spinning
Clouds gather
Huddle close
Does this day matter?

See my face- twisted words unspoken
Desire to stop the spin
My mind pretends it is broken
More convoluted that it has ever been.

In the unstable stillness
I wonder aloud
Did my face shine for even a moment
Make you sad or perhaps proud??

# Cleaning Out My Gutters

Gutters- clearing out the soul of season's past.
Seasons last?
Paint my face with the discarded mud and leaves
of yesterday's chaos.
Fresh in my mind- as the promise of spring will
be
Soon.
Let the November moonlight guide (chide) me
As I descend the ladder
Careful to avoid the missteps of past mentors.
Wave to the inquisitive dogs & fading daylight
Watching pretentiously from afar.
Guide my lustful spirit.
Prove to be a trustworthy servant
State my testimony- if only you'd hear it.

Gutters- empty as the winter air that silently
approaches
I can smell the change out amongst the
Broken promises of a summer pact
Recently fractured with expected irony
Summon the will to repair- for I stare at every
crack.
My will for this work shall be steady, yet tested.
Fade into the premature night

Fearful that I will emerge properly rested.
For the gutters may never back up again
Agonizing, I'll still ascend the unsteady ladder
Emerge at the top and call you friend.

# Take That Crown

Brought down into the storm
Of self-judgment.  Worth.
Work.  A body desperately in need of
reinforcement.
Relevance.
Strength existing in areas of the mind and body
Previously dormant- or simply unfulfilled.

Awake.  Blood flowing as ink.
Tattoo your work. Words permanent-
and singular.
Uniquely talented, simply under-utilized.
Circle the day, not the frayed drain.
The unexpected hour has arrived.
Unannounced- but not unprepared.
Strength jolted to the surface.
King or Queen for the moment.
Take the crown and learn as you shine.
Leave the worry with the disposable heroes.

# Trampoline

Emotions bouncing on an under-sized
trampoline
Landing awkwardly, with massive internal force
Little chance to escape the constant (re)actions.
Deliberate movement across the unsteady
surface.
Dropping, crawling
    Desperation driving the fragile fingers
Searching for a Spring
That may bloom too late
Fragile nerves abandoned the Fall
In favor of the gate.

# Runaway Field

Runaway Field-
Only visible by the passing lights of careless
motorists.
Just another parcel left to wallow
Where life used to be full and fleeting
If only time had made those feelings solvent in
the moment.
Unkept and dormant for nearly a decade.

Michael found this to be his safe space.
Green blades to call own his own (greater than
silver).
He appreciated the natural feel of his
surroundings.
Open solitude only a child of age could
appreciate.
A certain unusual, unexpected feeling of privacy
Gave his mind the freedom to express ALL
No need to pretend in the present
Or let his thoughts stall.

The moonlight on this unusually cool July night
Highlighted his features so often overlooked
Self-reflection over self-infliction.
Appreciate, not analyze, for his weathered eyes-

Free of judgment.
Fatigue had unintentional inspiration.
A moment alone meant far more than the
meditation.
A field of opportunities he had long trusted to be
possible.

# Blue Cooler

I use my blue cooler to store my emotions away.
A daily dumpster of sorts
To keep unsteady thoughts at bay.
Fill it with ICE.
Though little need for it to remain chilled.
Rather, I wish for the ice to thaw and
contemplate
How those flawed cubes landed in this confined,
finite space-
Four white walls with little to offer, other than
solace.

Move my blue cooler-
  store in the unfamiliar corner.
Windowless, colorless, without purpose.
Sit and melt.
My mind paints a thousand images from the day
Yet in my heart, there are simmering emotions
not yet dealt.

Tomorrow, my blue cooler will be empty again
(my hope)
Dried out and void of validity.
My actions & acrimony will decide if it shall be
filled again.

Half-full of cold feelings
Or just idle.
And the day will evolve into beauty.
Yet the blue cooler will always remain
On stand by-
    for the next cold front that invades the tired
soul
The psyche that occasionally struggles
To maintain calamity and control.

# Stadium View

Her heart skipped a beat
As she leapt up in the heat.
Unwilling to contain the raw emotion
Of paradise found, if but for one day.

A mind at work sought to find the words
proper and present inside her heart.
Down near the hole for far too many moments
All that erased
An uprising so deserving
Yet her self-esteem still wavered.
Were events as they seem?

The open, frayed book sat near her feet.
Words nearly 36 years of age
Influenced her present decisions
As she swiftly scanned from page to blurry page.
A moment of intense clarity.
She glared at the simple pink spot near the bottom
of her sometimes sweet sundress.
Stood and spoke with poise
Her life filled with swift, tangible rewards.
New beginnings-
Altered the landscape of her stadium view.

The trouble that suddenly looked lost in the distance.

# Gassed

Both feet firmly on the throttle
Until he could hold it steady no more
One hand still clutching the unsteady wheel
While the other mischievously inched toward
the door.

See the station with a wandering eye
Thoughts escaping through his fatigued lenses
How to adjust- without saying goodbye.
Re-consider or Re-charge?

Road in the rear view-
Full of slush and potholes (none avoided).
Unrelenting sleet as far as his vision could
muster
Was it time to increase his wipers
Or cut the engine & prepare to sell??

Pulled over to the side.
A quick, calculated exhale
Not his place to hide
Or idle, as his engine was with the patience he
yearned for.

One foot slowly inched back to the peddle

A mental reset while at the yellow curb
Not one to let his attitude often meddle
A sweep to the left
With both hands now firmly clutching the wheel
As he kept his speed
Slower, yet steady.
And the clouds, so stubborn in his mind
Began to clear.

# Grounded Love

She loves the ground she stands on.
Carolyn is firm when she feels strongly about
her convictions.
Sometimes mushy-
        as she works it out in her mind.
Soft when the need is present
To let someone in that may be lost.
Pay it forward
When there was never an act to reciprocate.

The ground often shifts without the critical
knowledge
Of the people it supports.
She is always a step ahead of her peers
The planned earthquake that strikes so many
And is often unforgiving in force and frustration.

Her ground is solid
And she has worked to maintain that foundation
In every aspect of her day
While always moving forward
Surviving the storm(s) while finding her way.

# Invited

Invited-
without proper warning, nor time
To prepare.
The chase,
          scramble
Organize thoughts to be accepted in the present
tense.

Hurried.  Worried?  Let your mind twirl around
the imagination pole.
Will you accept the minor marathon
Thoughts preparing- waiting to go.
Present tense.
Sometimes slight warning
Controls the present(s)
Makes that work oddly relevant, yet restless.

A room with a minimal view
Cloudy skies match the judgment
Of worth & willpower
But passion for paper testimony
Jolted into the wilting flowers
Long gone to the hands of fall
United they became Invited
And stood again- willful and tall.

A sudden burst of beauty bleeding with
Creativity-
    at the curiosity
Of the assignment (or the assessment).
Adjust- and trust- Always
Invited
Question the reason
Accept willingly
Extension of the season.


A lap not of luxury but of grounded
                            grace.